HAWKS EAT

GINA CLINE
TRACI DIBBLE

See this bird? It's a hawk.

Hawks eat animals.

Hawks eat fish.

4

Hawks eat lizards.

Hawks eat birds, too.

Hawks love to eat rabbits.

This hawk wants to get a rabbit.

She looks for a rabbit from a tree.

A rabbit runs across the snow.

The hawk flies down.

She flies over the snow.

She goes down to get the rabbit.

13

These are the hawk's claws.

The hawk gets the rabbit with her claws.

This is the hawk's beak.

She eats the rabbit with her beak.

Here comes a new hawk.

He sees the hawk with the rabbit.

He wants to eat the rabbit, too.

The hawks will fight.

Who will get the rabbit?

23

Power Words
How many can you read?

a	he	the
animal	her	these
are	is	this
come	it's	to
down	look	too
eat	love	want
for	new	who
from	over	will
get	see	with
goes	she	